PRACTICAL
MAGIC

for Kids

PRACTICAL MAGIC FOR KIDS

Your Guide to
CRYSTALS, HOROSCOPES, DREAMS, AND MORE

NIKKI VAN DE CAR
Illustrated by **KATIE VERNON**

RP|KIDS
PHILADELPHIA

Running Press Kids
Hachette Book Group
1290 Avenue of the Americas, New York, NY 10104
www.runningpress.com/rpkids
@RP_Kids

Printed in China

First Edition: October 2022

Published by Running Press Kids, an imprint of Perseus Books, LLC,
a subsidiary of Hachette Book Group, Inc. The Running Press Kids name
and logo is a trademark of the Hachette Book Group.

The Hachette Speakers Bureau provides a wide range of authors
for speaking events. To find out more, go to www.hachettespeakersbureau.com
or call (866) 376-6591.

The publisher is not responsible for websites (or their content)
that are not owned by the publisher.

Print book cover and interior design by Frances J. Soo Ping Chow.

Library of Congress Control Number: 2021952292

ISBNs: 978-0-7624-8130-9 (hardcover), 978-0-7624-8131-6

APS

10   9   8   7   6   5   4   3   2   1

CONTENTS

INTRODUCTION

• •

HAVE YOU EVER WONDERED WHAT YOUR FUTURE MIGHT HOLD?
Have you stared at the lines on your palm, tracing them and trying to find
the path to the person you're meant to be? What was the universe trying
to tell you with that strange dream last night? And what *are* chakras all
about, anyway?

This book is for anyone who has always wanted to live in a world
full of magic and possibility. Here you'll learn the basics of crystal healing, herb magic, and palm-reading. You'll learn how to cast a few basic
spells, how to see auras, and how to choose a crystal that will give you
extra energy. You'll learn how to interpret your dreams, to balance your
chakras, and even to chart your stars.

The truth is, there is a whole lot of magic in the world.

But what exactly do we mean by *magic*? Is it the slow opening of
a flower or a fern? Is it the kind act we do for someone we don't really
know? Is it the creation of something that wasn't there before—like a
painting or a story or even just an idea?

Absolutely! All of that is magic. And then there's the magic we look
for and bring out in the world, just by seeking and exploring and setting
our intentions for good. This kind of magic is something you can create
for yourself—all you need is a little imagination and a sense of curiosity.

Let's explore.

PART 1

· · · · · · · · · · · · · · · ✶ · · · · · · · · · · · ·

HEALING

CHAKRAS

• •

FOR OUR FIRST LESSON ON HEALING, LET'S GO RIGHT TO THE source—all healing starts with your body and its energy centers. Have you heard of *chakras* before? Depending on your background the idea of chakras can seem very familiar, or maybe a little confusing.

Maybe you already know that chakras are all about energy and how it flows through your body, but aren't sure what it really means to have spinning multicolored spirals at different points in your body.

Let's think about it. There are all sorts of energies throughout the universe—solar energy, magnetic energy, gravity, and the list goes on and on. It makes sense that you have a type of energy in your body, too! A chakra is just an energy center in your body. When you try to picture your chakras, think of them as wheels or swirls found in specific places along your spine. (Chakras are a concept that comes from different cultural traditions, too, mostly from Asia, so the word *chakra* is Sanskrit for "wheel.") Each of these are connected to the others by something known as *prana* or *qi*—which is basically our life force.

So how do the chakras work? Inside each of us there are seven main chakras, and for your body, mind, and spirit to be whole, each of these chakras needs to be open and balanced. Sometimes a chakra's connection to the body might not be working so well, and that can lead to a hard time with thoughts or feelings. But the opposite is also true! If a chakra's

5

connection is working exceptionally well, you can feel perfectly aligned with the thoughts or feelings associated with that energy center.

If you're having thoughts or feelings connected to one of your chakras that are a little bit tough, you might feel a reaction in your body. Remember: Your body is not separate from your mind and spirit—all of them combine to make you who you are.

Sometimes, a chakra can get out of balance, meaning it's working too hard—which we call "overactive"—or it's stuck and can't let energy move—which we call "blocked." A blocked chakra stops your prana (remember, that means your personal energy) from moving through it, while an overactive chakra can crowd out the others, making itself your only focus. Just as each part of your body works for the whole, each chakra responds to the others. If one is out of balance, the others feel it too. For your body, mind, and spirit to be in tune, your chakras need to be balanced.

A chakra that is balanced flows freely, back and forth like the tides, and that flow actually makes a sound! Each chakra has its very own sound (called a frequency) as well as its own color (called a light frequency). These sounds and colors are special, even magical, because we can use them to open or close our chakras when we feel a little out of balance. When all your chakras are in balance, you will feel comfortable and at ease within your whole self.

THE SEVEN CHAKRAS

Muladhara

The root chakra is located at the base of the spine. It is the most basic of all chakras—our fight-or-flight response is located here. It is our connection with the past, with our ancestral memories, and it establishes our deepest connection with the earth. When this chakra is balanced, we feel completely fearless and safe, but if we're feeling worried every day, that may mean the root chakra is out of balance.

COLOR: red ✦ ESSENTIAL OILS: cedar, clove, myrrh ✦ SOUND: LAM ✦
CRYSTALS: agate, bloodstone, bronzite, hematite,
obsidian, smoky quartz

Svadhisthana

The sacral chakra is right above the root chakra, just below your belly button, and it's the source of your creativity and pleasure. When this chakra is balanced, we are brimming with ideas and imagination. But if the sacral chakra is out of balance, we might feel distracted or may be bored with things we normally enjoy.

COLOR: orange ✦ ESSENTIAL OILS: sandalwood,
ylang-ylang ✦ SOUND: VAM ✦ CRYSTALS: carnelian,
citrine, garnet, ruby, rutilated quartz, sunstone

Manipura

✦

The solar plexus chakra is found just above the belly button, and it represents our inner strength. It is all about confidence! If your solar plexus chakra is out of balance, you might be afraid of being rejected or told you're wrong—or you might be feeling stressed and more emotional than usual.

COLOR: **yellow** ✦ ESSENTIAL OILS: **chamomile, lemon** ✦ SOUND: **RAM** ✦
CRYSTALS: **mookaite, peridot, pyrite, tigereye, yellow jasper**

Anahata

✦

The heart chakra is found in the center of your chest. It is the link between the other chakras, keeping them all in balance. And what's a better way to find balance than through love? That includes any kind of love—romantic, friendship, kindness, and loving yourself. When this chakra is out of balance, we can feel very lonely.

COLOR: **green** ✦
ESSENTIAL OILS: **bergamot, rose** ✦
SOUND: **YAM** ✦ CRYSTALS: **emerald, malachite, morganite, rhodonite, rose quartz**

Vishuddha

Located right at the base of your throat, this chakra is all about speaking out and standing up for what you believe in. It helps us speak the truth, and it can also help us hear it. When the throat chakra is out of balance, we might be afraid of rejection or find ourselves talking without listening.

COLOR: **light blue** ✦ ESSENTIAL OILS: **lavender, neroli, sage** ✦
SOUND: **HAM** ✦ CRYSTALS: **aquamarine, blue lace agate,
sodalite, turquoise**

Ajna

The third eye chakra is about seeing things clearly. It is located just between your eyebrows, and it helps you see everything that is happening around you—including the experiences and emotions of other people (even when they aren't telling you about them!). This chakra can help us understand what other people are going through, and when it's out of balance, we can feel cut off from the world.

COLOR: **indigo** ✦ ESSENTIAL OILS: **jasmine,
rosemary, vetiver** ✦ SOUND: **OHM** ✦
CRYSTALS: **apophyllite, azurite, fluorite, fuchsite,
labradorite, lapis lazuli, lepidolite, sapphire**

Sahasrara

The crown chakra is located at the very top of the head. If you are looking for the magic in chakras, it's here! This chakra helps you find and use your intuition—that ability you have to sense things even when you can't explain them. The crown chakra helps us understand how we are all connected.

COLOR: **purple** ✦ ESSENTIAL OILS: **frankincense, olibanum** ✦ SOUND: **OHM** ✦ CRYSTALS: **amethyst, apophyllite, celestite, clear quartz, kyanite, opal, sugilite**

BALANCING YOUR CHAKRAS ALL TOGETHER

The best way to bring your chakras into balance with one another is through meditation. Meditation can seem really intimidating and complicated, but I promise, it's not! It's just about sitting quietly and letting yourself *be*. Sit comfortably, and don't try to not think about anything at all—that's impossible! Instead, just notice the thoughts that come, and let them drift away, while staying relaxed and peaceful.

When you feel calm, pay attention to your root chakra. Imagine its color, and picture its swirl of energy flowing in and out of you. Take a deep breath and chant "LAM," drawing it out like *"laaaaaaahhhhhmmmmmmm."*

Keep going just like this with all of your chakras, paying attention to each one in turn as you move up your body. See each chakra's color in your mind, and chant its sound aloud—don't worry about feeling silly! When you've finished, imagine yourself surrounded by a glow of white light. Maybe whisper to yourself, "I am calm," or "I am complete." Take a few deep breaths, and let the energy of your chakras settle.

BALANCING THE INDIVIDUAL CHAKRAS

Meditation can also help balance a particular chakra if it doesn't feel quite right—you can also use the crystals and essential oils for that chakra (see pages 7–10) to help you. Try resting the crystal on the chakra if you're lying down, or you can also simply hold the crystal in your hand.

But if meditation doesn't feel right to you, you can also try these methods of balancing the chakras.

Muladhara

Look for the color red, particularly in your food. Let your bare feet feel the earth. Do something practical, like cleaning up your bedroom or doing a little schoolwork. Use this chakra's oils in a footbath (you can fill a nice deep bowl with warm water and a bit of the oil), or apply a warm cloth with a few drops of oil to the base of your spine.

Svadhisthana

Eat orange foods, and do something that makes you happy—especially something creative! Drop some essential oils in a bath or shower, or ask an adult if you can use a scented candle.

Manipura

Get some sunshine! Go to the beach if you can, or if the weather isn't right, just curl up indoors near a window. Eat yellow foods, including lots of citrus, drink some chamomile tea, and give yourself a lot of love.

Anahata

Make time for the people you love! Hang out with friends and family—all the love you feel for them will come right back to you. And while you're at it, eat lots of leafy greens.

Vishuddha

Write in a journal—you might even try writing some poetry. Maybe even sing! Look for the color blue . . . there aren't many blue foods, but you could wear a blue shirt, or simply notice the blue you see around you, whether it's the sky or a flower or a picture.

Ajna

Try to listen closely when others are speaking. Read about what is going on in the world and ask questions. Wear dark blue, and close your eyes so that you can think about what you have seen and heard.

Sahasrara

For this one, you really should meditate, if you can. Ask the universe for guidance, and listen for an answer. Look for purple around you. Imagine all the possibilities in the world, and even reflect on what might seem *impossible*. Let yourself daydream.

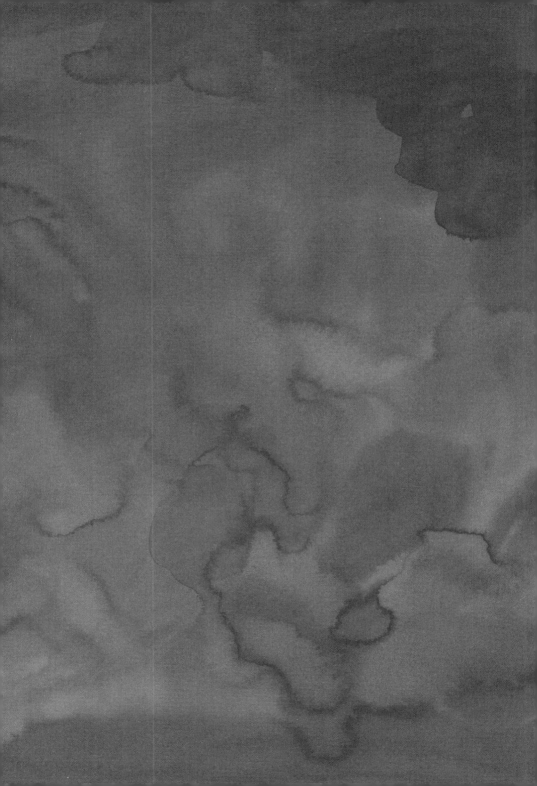

PERIDOT

CeLeSTITe

CARNeLIAN

FLUORITE

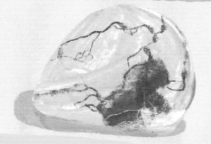

HOWLITe

CRYSTALS

· ·

WORKING WITH CRYSTALS IS SOMETHING PEOPLE HAVE DONE for thousands of years, all over the world! Some people say that crystal healing has been around for 6,000 years, starting with the ancient Egyptians. Hawaiians have a stone-based healing practice, as do the Hopi, though the crystal healing you know today is most tied to the Buddhist and Hindu understanding of chakras. All of these practices give different meanings to different stones—diamonds to help draw out poison, garnets to keep nightmares away, jade for long life, and so on.

Because there are so many stones with so many varied uses, crystal healing can be kind of complicated—but that's also what makes it magical. The power of each crystal changes not just with its type but also its shape. Rose quartz, for example, will lead to different results if it's shaped like a wand or just a tumbled stone.

THE MOST COMMON STONES AND THEIR USES

AGATE ◆ Courage, strength, and self-confidence.

AMAZONITE ◆ Helps fight blue moods during the winter and can make you more of a leader.

AMETHYST ◆ Intuition, meditation, and calm. Relieves headaches.

APOPHYLLITE ◆ A calming stone that balances the third eye and crown chakras, releasing stress.

AQUAMARINE ◆ Helps you speak your truth. Reduces fear and tension.

AVENTURINE ◆ A "stone of opportunity" that brings luck and wealth.

AZURITE ◆ Changes fear into understanding.

BLACK TOURMALINE ◆ A stone of protection.

BLOODSTONE ◆ Helps you find your inner strength and courage.

BLUE LACE AGATE ◆ This gentle stone of communication can help you let go of anger and tension.

BRONZITE ◆ Energizes and protects, so you have the strength you need to handle any challenges.

CALCITE ◆ An energy magnifier, it makes it easier to communicate with the spiritual world.

CARNELIAN ◆ For creativity.

CELESTITE ◆ Helps you stand back and look at a problem without feeling emotional.

CHRYSOCOLLA ◆ Also known as the Goddess Stone, chrysocolla helps you tap into your feminine power.

CITRINE ◆ A stone of plenty, it brings success and money, and raises your self-esteem.

CLEAR QUARTZ ◆ A stone of healing, clear quartz can also do whatever you need it to.

EMERALD ◆ This "stone of successful love" encourages you to give love and feel it in return.

FLUORITE ◆ Helps with decisions and concentration.

GARNET ◆ A stone of health and creativity. Helps stop nightmares.

HEMATITE ◆ A stone of protection, it closes your aura to keep out negative energy.

HOWLITE ◆ Eases anger, so you can have a calm heart and a clear mind.

JADE ◆ Will help you work for what you want. Good for long life.

KYANITE ◆ Encourages communication and psychic ability.

LAPIS LAZULI ◆ A stone of focus that helps with meditation and releases you from sadness.

MERLINITE ◆ A "stone of storms," merlinite can help you move forward after you've been hurt.

MOONSTONE ◆ Encourages peace and harmony within.

OBSIDIAN ◆ A stone of protection, it will help you to understand and face your deepest fears.

OPAL ◆ A stone that increases your power, opal can make your creativity stronger. Balances mood swings.

PERIDOT ◆ Symbolizes the sun, and invites energy, positivity, and light.

PYRITE ◆ A stone of defense and protection, it also symbolizes the sun.

RHODOCHROSITE ◆ For self-love.

ROSE QUARTZ ◆ A stone of love, but not just romantic love: it enhances friend-love and family-love, too.

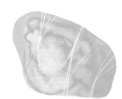

RUTILATED QUARTZ ◆ This type of quartz has golden streaks known as "angel threads" or "Venus hairs." It helps fight sadness.

SELENITE ◆ A form of gypsum crystals often shaped like a wand, selenite is used to get rid of negative energy.

SMOKY QUARTZ ◆ A stone of protection, it boosts your survival instincts and helps you feel more focused.

SODALITE ◆ A "stone of truth," sodalite will help you speak your truths and understand and accept the truths of others.

SUNSTONE ◆ A happy stone that helps energy move freely through the body.

TIGEREYE ◆ A stone of strength, tigereye can help you feel more powerful.

TURQUOISE ◆ A stone of healing.

HOW TO CHOOSE AND ACTIVATE YOUR CRYSTAL

The first step is to figure out what you need from your crystal. Do you want to boost your intuition? Do you want to cast a spell? Maybe you feel drawn to a particular stone, almost as if it's choosing you, rather than the other way around. And if you're not sure, try clear quartz! It can do whatever you need it to.

Once you have an idea of the type of stone you want to work with, you need to choose its shape. The following sections will give you some ideas on where you can find stones of different shapes.

WAND ◆ This type of crystal, rough at one end and pointed at the other, is often found in jewelry, but the shape can help you direct the crystal's energies in a more specific way.

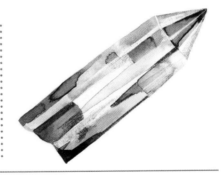

CHUNK ◆ This is a crystal that's kind of lumpy—turquoise often comes in this form, as does pyrite. You might see these placed around a home or office to cleanse negative energy. Mineral and curio shops will have this kind of stone and also may carry all the other kinds, too.

CUT ✦ This is when a crystal or gem has been shaped to enhance sparkle and capture light, which increases the crystal's energies. Cut crystals are also often used in jewelry.

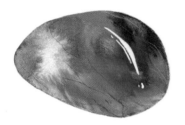

TUMBLED ✦ These are the stones you'll find in bins at a science or mystical shop. They are smooth, shiny, and comforting to hold.

Once you've chosen a stone, the next thing you'll want to do is clear it. What does that mean, exactly? Well, your stone didn't come to you straight from the earth—it was found by others and handled by others, and they've given it their energy. Before you use your stone, you want to clean that energy off, so it is ready to help *you*. There are a few ways to do that: you can soak it in salt water or hold it under running water—rain or even your faucet will work. Those are the simplest ways, but if your stone needs a gentler touch, you can let it rest a while with carnelian or clear quartz, which can do the cleansing for you. You can also let sunlight or moonlight work their magic by letting your stone bathe in their rays for a while.

Once the stone is cleared, it can be activated. Each stone has its own special meaning, but you can focus that energy by telling it what you need it to do. This can be as simple as holding the crystal in your hand and setting an intention by thinking about what you want it to do. Or you can really set the stage by performing a ritual.

Stand in the light—either sunlight or moonlight will work—and hold the crystal so that the light shines on it. You can say you intention out loud, or you can just think it to yourself. Hold the crystal to your heart and bow your head in thanks.

KETHERIC TEMPLATE AURA

CELESTIAL AURA

ETHERIC TEMPLATE AURA

ASTRAL AURA

MENTAL AURA

EMOTIONAL AURA

ETHERIC AURA

AURAS

· ·

HAVE YOU EVER HAD A MOMENT WHERE SOMEONE FELT SO CLOSE to you it was uncomfortable? I bet so—most of us have! It's like when you're in an elevator or out on the street, and it feels like someone touched your shoulder—even though they didn't. Everyone gets that uncomfortable sensation from time to time.

But it also works the other way—sometimes just being near someone we love, or whose energy feels good to us, can be comforting, letting us feel warmth and happiness down to our bones. We can call that invisible something around us our "space," our "bubble," our "energy field," but the spiritual word for it is our *aura*.

All living things have an aura around them, which usually spreads about three feet away from their body. Try rubbing your palms together really fast, until you feel them getting warm. Then stop and let them move slowly apart, paying attention to the energy you feel between your palms and the heat. You are feeling your own aura. Isn't it magical?

All the energy that we have flowing in our bodies is concentrated in the chakras, but it also goes all over. It even flows outside of us, so that whatever we are feeling inside spills out around us on the outside, too. If we are out of balance, someone who can read auras can see that. In fact, we all read people's auras all the time without knowing it! Maybe there was a time when your dad snapped at you, even though you didn't do anything wrong. At first you might have been upset, but when you thought about what was really going on, you figured out that he was actually on edge about work. You didn't need him to tell you that—you could just tell from his body and face—and maybe also from a sense you couldn't quite name. That unnameable sense is reading auras.

An aura has seven layers called the "subtle bodies." These layers change depending on how the person is feeling—so someone's aura doesn't always look the same and is not always the same color. Let's look at the different layers.

ETHERIC AURA ✦ This layer is the closest to your body, going only one to two inches outside your skin. It holds information about how you're feeling physically. Its color is typically blue, but it can look gray if you are more active, like if you play sports a lot.

EMOTIONAL AURA ✦ This layer reaches three inches from your body. The emotional aura can be any color and can have spots or patches that show different feelings. If your feelings are confused, your aura will look muddy.

MENTAL AURA ✦ This layer reaches eight inches from your body. If you are deep in thought, this layer will look bright yellow, with colors standing out depending on what you're thinking and feeling.

ASTRAL AURA ✦ So the first three aural layers are connections to what is going on inside us that generally make sense, but starting here, things get a little wild. The astral aura shows your *higher self*—you can think of that as the best version of yourself, the person you try to be every day. When we feel love of any kind, it glows pink. This layer reaches about a foot away from your body.

ETHERIC TEMPLATE AURA ✦ This layer reaches about two feet from your body and basically represents who you are, deep down.

CELESTIAL AURA ✦ This layer reaches about two and a half feet from your body. Its colors are usually sparkling soft pastels, and it shows your connection with all the magic in the world.

KETHERIC TEMPLATE AURA ✦ This is where we can find our intuition—our way of knowing things that we can't really explain. It reaches about three feet from your body and shines like a web of gold.

Even though we can all sense auras, we are not all able to sense every layer, at least not on their own—only very practiced aura readers can do that. Once we've taught ourselves to actually see the auras, not just sense them, we still have a hard time understanding them. That's because the layers lie on top of one another, so that we see them all blended together. But this still gives us a lot of information! An aura is hardly ever just one color, but usually there's one color that stands out the most. If that color is clear and bright, we think of the aura as healthy, but if it is muddy, the person may be feeling some confusion and dealing with some tough feelings at that moment.

HOW TO SEE AURAS

First, get comfortable *sensing* auras. We all do this without thinking about it, so all you need to do is pay more attention. Take a look at some-one sitting near you, and try to figure them out. Use all of your senses, if you can—what do they look like, sound like, smell like? What do you *feel* about them? Then, decide what color that person should be. Don't think about the meaning of the color, just listen to your instincts and intuition.

Next, try using your peripheral vision, or what you can see out of the sides of your eyes, without looking directly at them. Out of the sides of our eyes we often half-see things that aren't really there—or at least aren't always visible . . . If you look at the person out of the corner of your eye, do you sense a color? With practice, you can develop your peripheral vision.

Finally, ask the person to stand in front of a white wall, and sway gently from side to side. Let your eyes get blurry. Don't scrunch up your eyes—this isn't something that requires good eyesight, as it isn't really about *seeing* at all. Any colors that you pick up on the white wall will tell you about the person's aura.

COMMON AURAL COLORS AND THEIR MEANINGS

Red

A red aura can be a little hard to make sense of, because it can be either positive or negative. Check your own feelings about the person's aura to help you figure that out. Red can mean healthy pride, or it can mean anger and anxiety.

DARK RED. Usually means someone with a strong sense of who they are.
MUDDY RED. Means the person is angry.
BRIGHT RED. Passionate, competitive, and energetic.
PINK. Artistic and loving.
MUDDY PINK. Means they might be lying to themselves or others.

Orange

An orange aura usually means that the person is healthy and full of energy.

RED ORANGE. Means the person is confident.
YELLOW ORANGE. This person is creative and smart.
MUDDY ORANGE. This person is feeling lazy.

Yellow

This person is full of life and fun.

PASTEL YELLOW. This person usually looks on the bright side.
BRIGHT YELLOW. This person has trouble feeling powerful.
MUDDY YELLOW. They may be tired from trying to do too much all at once.

Green

Many teachers and healers have green auras, as do people who work with nature. It is the color of love and healing. Someone with a green aura works to help the world in whatever way they can.

YELLOW GREEN. Good at communication.
BRIGHT GREEN. Natural healer.
MUDDY GREEN. This person might be feeling jealous or insecure.

Blue

People with blue auras are calm, sensitive, and intuitive.

TURQUOISE. Powerful healer.
LIGHT BLUE. Truthful and peaceful.
BRIGHT BLUE. This person might be able to read others'
thoughts or futures.
MUDDY BLUE. This person might be lying,
but it's because they are afraid.

Purple

People with purple auras are very spiritual and
possess extraordinary gifts.

BLUE-VIOLET. A wonderful daydreamer.
This person can make the world the way they wish it to be.
VIOLET. Very powerful and wise.
LAVENDER. Imaginative and creative.
MUDDY VIOLET. This person's gifts are being blocked,
probably by their own self-doubt.

HOW TO CLEANSE
YOUR AURA

Cleansing your aura is not that different from balancing your chakras, but you need to do it more often because auras are touched by the outside world more than your chakras are. Just brushing up against a negative aura can make you start to feel negative, too. So if you find yourself in a bad mood all of a sudden—or if you're having a good time with your friends and suddenly everything goes wrong for no reason—that can be because of someone else's aura brushing up against yours.

You can cleanse your aura by doing the chakra-balancing ritual (see page 10) and then protecting your aura from outside energies. While you're meditating, imagine a wall around you. It's a special kind of wall that can let in whatever you want and keep out whatever you don't want. It can close out anger while still welcoming in love and positivity.

There are also cords that bind us to everyone around us—thick, strong cords between us and those we love the most and thin threads that connect strangers. Those threads can always grow back, but sometimes you need some space from other people. Imagine breaking those threads, and then imagine the thick, strong cords that connect you to the people you love getting a little looser. Don't worry, though! They're still there, so you're still connected, but they aren't pulling at you so hard. If there is a cord that needs to be broken—say, attaching to a friend who isn't good for you—imagine that happening, too.

If you feel like you have too much going on, picture your aura pulling in toward you, keeping your energy close to your heart.

Water is another good way to clean off you aura, particularly moving water like a stream, a waterfall, or the ocean. You can also try taking a saltwater bath with some crystals nearby. And you can even carry those crystals with you as amulets for added protection for your aura.

PART 2

MAGIC

ROSE

MULLEIN

CALENDULA

LEMON
BALM

PLANT-BASED MAGIC

• •

PEOPLE HAVE BEEN USING PLANTS FOR HEALING MAGIC FOR HUN-
dreds of years. It's true! You probably already do it more than you realize.
Have you ever had a cup of chamomile tea when you're feeling upset?
That's a healing potion! And plant magic doesn't always have to be something you eat or drink. You can make lotions or balms or keep special
plants in your room—a little lavender plant can help you feel more
peaceful, or a mint plant can help you feel more focused.

Think about it—what could be more powerful, more magical, than
working with the earth and the life around us to make ourselves feel
better? Some of the ingredients that we read about witches using—
things like "eye of newt" and "toe of frog"—were actually folk names for
plants. Eye of newt is just another name for mustard seed, and frog's feet
were buttercups. Some people think these folk names were really code
names that witches used to keep their potion recipes secret, while having
a good laugh about some poor fool running off to risk his life for a wolf's
claw . . . when all he really needed was some moss.

But what is all this mustard seed and moss
supposed to do? Well, just like with everything
else in this book, it's about *energy*. Like the
chakras and the crystals (see pages 5 and 15),
plant magic is about bringing your body, mind,

and spirit into balance. You can use the plants in the same way you do the crystals and the chakras—by directing your energy in a positive, loving way.

Plant-based magic isn't so much about casting spells—it's more about using plants in thoughtful, special ways. Keeping certain plants around your house, eating or burning them (with the help of grown-ups, always!), or even carrying them around your neck in a small bag—these are all great ways to bring plant magic into your life.

COMMON PLANTS AND THEIR USES IN MAGIC

Remember to always ask for help from adults when you are using plants for magic, especially any that you might want to eat, drink, or take from the outdoors. We always have to be careful of poisonous plants and parts of plants when we are interacting with nature.

BETONY ◆ For protection. Stops nightmares, and can help with a headache or if you have trouble sleeping. You shouldn't eat betony, but we'll use it later in herbal bundles and branches placed as protection.

CALENDULA ◆ Also known as marigold, it's good for the skin, can calm an upset stomach, and helps with divination. It can be used in lotion directly on the skin and is safe to drink as a tea.

CARAWAY ◆ Often used in baking and cooking, caraway tastes a little like licorice. It gives a sense of well-being and helps you think clearly.

CHAMOMILE ◆ This soothing herb is delicious in tea, and it makes you feel peaceful and calm. Can help with meditation and rest.

EYEBRIGHT ◆ You can make a balm and rub on your third eye, but don't eat it!

FRANKINCENSE ◆ This is often made into an essential oil, and it can help with meditation, as we saw with the crown chakra. Do not eat.

GARLIC ◆ Protection, healing, and courage. Plus it's tasty and good for you!

HOLLY ◆ Powerful protection against evil. You can use this nonedible plant in herbal bundles and place the branches around you for protection. Do not eat.

LAVENDER ◆ Helps you think clearly, and is good for peace and protection. It's safe and soothing to eat.

LEMON BALM ◆ Also known as "melissa," this member of the mint family smells a bit like lemons. It can help you feel happier, calm any stress, and assist you in thinking clearly. It's safe and yummy to eat.

MINT ◆ Very tasty and safe to eat, mint gives you energy, helps with clear thinking, and offers good luck!

MUGWORT ◆ The go-to herb for witches! Using this nonedible plant in things like charm bags helps you feel your own power and gives you energy. Do not eat.

MULLEIN ◆ Mullein is great if you have a cold, and it can help if your head aches. You might like this as a tea with lots of lemon and honey.

ROSE ◆ It's great for the skin and for love. Safe to drink as tea or to use in a balm.

ROSEMARY ◆ Think "rosemary for remembrance." This delicious herb helps with memory and clear thinking.

SAGE ◆ Also delicious, this herb can help you pay attention and feel wise.

THYME ◆ Gives you energy, purifies the spirit, and is very tasty.

YARROW ◆ Can help you see things you might not always notice. Safe to drink as a tea.

HOW TO MAKE AN HERBAL OIL

Did you know that you can make your own magic oils? The nice thing about doing so is that you can use any herbs you like. You might mix calendula, lemon balm, rose, and mullein for an oil that is great for your skin and your emotions, or you can combine lavender, lemon balm, and mint for a calm oil to rub next to your ears when you're feeling anxious.

Carefully chop or mash up your chosen herbs (asking an adult for help if you're using a knife), then place them in a jar. Fill the jar with an oil (olive or almond oil are two of my favorites), so that is covers the herbs by one inch, with one inch of space at the top. Close the jar tightly, and allow it to sit in sunshine for a month.

Pour the oil through a cheesecloth whenever you need it, leaving the rest to continue getting more powerful.

HOW TO MAKE AN HERBAL BUNDLE

An herbal bundle is a small bunch of wrapped plants that will be lit on fire to release their energies into the air. Normally herbal bundles are used to get rid of negative energy in a space, so you can make a cleansing stick out of sage and thyme, or a protective stick with some combination of holly, garlic, and betony. Or you can combine sage for wisdom with rosemary and mint for clear thinking.

You can use fresh or dried plants for your herbal bundle. Lay your choices together in a clump—you'll want to create a bundle that is at least five inches long, so that you can hold it comfortably while it burns. Use a cotton string to wrap the bundle into a firm stick, winding your way up and down the length of the stems—make sure you wrap it tightly. If you've used fresh plants, hang them upside down to dry for a week before burning.

Light the tip of your herbal bundle with a candle, getting assistance from adults if necessary. Once it has a steady flame, blow it out so that the bundle is just barely smoking, with plumes rising from the glowing tip. Fan the smoke over your head or around the room. (Be careful inhaling the smoke, particularly if you have asthma or any other respiratory issues.) To put out your herbal bundle, smother the flame by pushing it into a clear area of dirt outside—stay away from any plants that might catch on fire—or onto a plate. Try to avoid using water, since you won't be able to use your herbal bundle again if it gets wet—but don't hesitate to use water if you need to put any flames out fast.

HOW TO MAKE
A CHARM BAG

Charm bags let you keep a bit of magic with you, wherever you are. They are small enough to carry with you, or you can keep them under your pillow. You can even give them as gifts to your friends.

Begin by choosing the fabric for your bag. Leather, velvet, and felt are good choices, and they each have their own meanings. Velvet might make you think of being fancy and special, while leather might might make you think of strength or protection. Felt is the most common choice, because it is easy to find and use. The color of your fabric is also important, and you can use the colors of the chakras (see pages 7–10) to help you choose.

To create your bag, cut two, two- or three-inch squares of fabric and sew them together, leaving one side open. As you sew, think about what you want your charm bag to do. What are your intentions for it? Turn it inside out and fill the bag with herbs and crystals (see pages 37 and 16) that will match your intention.

Sew the opening of your bag closed. If you want, you can stitch on a ribbon so that it can be worn around your neck.

FOR COURAGE

Garlic, tigereye, and aquamarine in a yellow bag.

FOR LUCK

Mint, caraway, aventurine, and jade
in a green or red bag.

FOR MAGIC

Yarrow, mugwort, lavender, opal, lapis lazuli,
and calcite in a purple bag.

OCTOBER

SAMHAIN `31`

NOVEMBER

DECEMBER

`≈21` **YULE**

JANUARY

FEBRUARY

`2` **IMBOLC**

MARCH

OSTARA `≈20`

APRIL

MAY

`1` **BELTANE**

JUNE

`≈21` **LITHA**

JULY

AUGUST

`1-2`

LAMMAS

SEPTEMBER

`≈2`

MABON

MAGICAL
HOLIDAYS

• •

THERE ARE EIGHT TRADITIONAL MAGICAL HOLIDAYS. YOU'LL notice that many of them fall on or around other holidays you or your friends know. Some of them also happen at the same time as changes in the seasons, like the winter solstice (the longest night of the year) or when the earth lines up with stars or other planets in the solar system. They almost always have something to do with farming, because they were established back when everyone was growing their own food and their lives revolved around the harvest. Because of this, the dates of magical holidays can change—like when the longest night falls on December 22 one year and December 21 another. Sometimes we have to be a little flexible.

The traditions behind these days have been celebrated for thousands of years. They are meant to honor a certain time of the year—like harvest or spring—or to honor a god or goddess, usually from Celtic or Irish stories and myths—like Brighid, Lugh, or the Green Man. They are also times for reflection, when we can think about what we might have done in a different way and how we might continue to grow and change.

SAMHAIN

Pronounced SOW-in. Takes place on October 31.

So many cultures around the world have a day to honor and celebrate people who are no longer with us. There is the Bon Festival in Japan, Chuseok in Korea, the Festival of Cows in Nepal, the Ghost Festival in China, the Day of the Dead in Mexico, the Turning of the Bones in Madagascar—and, of course, Halloween. Death is a part of life, and all of these cultures know that it helps to have a sense of celebration and joy in something we might fear.

On Samhain, the laws of space and time are a little weaker, and whatever it is that separates life and death feels a little thinner. Maybe it's easier to talk to spirits on Samhain? Of course, that can be a little scary. Our celebrations of the dead are always a little spooky. It's a good idea to be extra careful on Samhain, so if you go out at night to trick-or-treat or see friends, carry a charm bag (see page 40).

WAYS TO CELEBRATE:

◆ Leave food or treats on your doorstep for the dead, who may be walking.

◆ Light a candle in your window to invite the spirits of your loved ones home. You can set an extra place at the dinner table for them, too.

◆ Bury apples on the side of the road for spirits that might not have a home to go to.

◆ Light an outdoor fire! If your family has an outdoor fireplace, fire pit or bowl, or chiminea, tonight may be the night to put it to use. Write your name on a stone and toss it in. Check the stone in the morning—is it cracked or burned? Let your intuition guide you and the stone might have something to tell you about what the next few months will be like for you.

YULE

*Pronounced YEW-ell. The longest night of the year.
Falls on the winter solstice, so on or around December 21.*

After Yule the days get longer. The sun rises earlier and stays with us later into the night. Many of the things that make us think of Christmas come from Yule, including Christmas trees, the Yule log, and wassailing—an old term for singing Christmas carols.

Of course, these traditions weren't exactly the same during Yule celebrations. A tree was never cut down—instead, people would bring branches inside to decorate with. And the Yule log wasn't just a decoration—it was taken very seriously. You couldn't buy a Yule log; it needed to be given as a gift from a neighbor or family member or harvested yourself. The log was made of ash, and it was *big*. Once it was placed in the fire, it was decorated with evergreens, holly, and ivy, splashed with cider, and dusted with flour—for light and life. Then it was set alight with a piece of last year's log, saved for just this purpose. The log would burn for 12 days . . . as in the 12 days of Christmas.

WAYS TO CELEBRATE:

◆ Learn some traditional wassails or carols, like "The Holly and the Ivy," "This Endris Night," or "Gloucestershire Wassail," by checking them out online and sing them to any nearby trees and fields.

◆ Decorate your home with mistletoe, holly, and ivy.

◆ Make your own version of a Yule log, like setting candles in a wood base and lighting them for 12 nights.

IMBOLC

Pronounced IM-bullug. Also called Candlemas or Brighid's Day. Over the years it has transformed into Valentine's Day. Takes place on or around February 2.

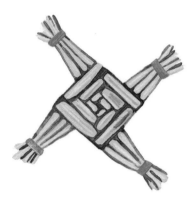

Imbolc is when we look forward to the end of winter and start to get ready for spring. Imbolc honors the goddess Brighid (pronounced Breej), the patron of fire, healing, and poetry—all things that we will be needing in the coming months.

Imbolc means it's time to clean your house. We don't have to stay inside, keeping warm from the cold winter, for much longer. It's time to *get to work.*

WAYS TO CELEBRATE:

◆ Go for a walk in the woods and look for flowers like crocuses or other signs of spring.

◆ Make a Brideo'gas—a little doll to honor Brighid. They're constructed from straw and decorated with bits of ribbon. You can put together your doll by making a figure out of two sticks tied together like a cross, then giving her a dress of straw and an acorn for a head. Then, lay her in your fireplace overnight. In the morning, take a look at the ashes to see if the doll left a mark—if it did, this will be a good season.

◆ Make a Brighid's Cross out of straw for protection.

◆ Light candles in your house (with an adult), to welcome the coming warmth.

OSTARA

Pronounced OH-star-ah. Celebrates the balance of night and day. Falls on the spring equinox, so on or around March 20.

There are a few gods and goddesses to celebrate on Ostara, but Eostre (pronounced EHS-truh) is the one that is the best known. Eggs and rabbits are her symbols . . . so that's where the Easter Bunny comes from.

Ostara also honors the Green Man, a mysterious figure found in a lot of different cultures around the world. Every year, he dies and is reborn, which represents the coming of spring. By now, spring has begun in earnest, and we can see it in the yellow-green leaves and the little buds that are popping up in the trees.

WAYS TO CELEBRATE:

- ◆ Coloring eggs is a way to celebrate Ostara, so have fun!
- ◆ Spend the day helping in your garden—if you don't have one, see if you can help at your neighborhood park.
- ◆ Go for a long hike in the woods.

BELTANE

Pronounced BAY al-TIN-uh. Falls on May 1.

Beltane is the most joyful holiday. It celebrates life, and how wonderful it is to *be* alive. Everything that feels good is a way to honor Beltane, whether you are smelling flowers on the breeze, rolling down a grassy hill, or spinning until you fall down.

WAYS TO CELEBRATE:

- ◆ Wake up early in the morning and collect flowers. Weave them into your hair.
- ◆ Collect wild water, like dew or fresh water from a stream, and wash your face with it.
- ◆ Build a small outdoor fire—be safe!—and tell stories around it.

LITHA

Pronounced LIE-tha. Also known as Midsummer Night's Eve.
Celebrated on the summer solstice, so on or near June 21.

This is another night of celebration, but there's a little less happy chaos than on Beltane. Litha is the shortest night of the year, and so it is a time to celebrate the sun and light. It's an opportunity to appreciate something we often take for granted—the miracle of light that we get to experience every day.

WAYS TO CELEBRATE:

◆ You can stay up late and notice how long—or short!—the night is, feeling grateful for the rest we get after the sun goes down.

◆ You can decorate your home with roses, which often bloom around Litha.

◆ Wake up early to watch the sun rise.

LAMMAS

Pronounced luh-MAHS. It is celebrated August 1–2.

Lammas is celebrated on the first harvest of the year—so right around the time you might start visiting the farmer's market with your family or friends. It is a sign that the hot days of summer are finally coming to an end. Lammas translates to "loaf-mass"—long ago, people placed loaves of bread on altars to honor the Green Man or the Sun God.

WAYS TO CELEBRATE:

- ◆ Bake a loaf of bread and share it with friends and family.
- ◆ Hold a feast, and maybe play some games! Board games or a game of catch or soccer are great ways to celebrate.
- ◆ Make a corn dolly out of a sheaf of corn and hang it in your room until the next harvest, when you can plant it to grow again.

MABON

Pronounced MAY-bun. It is held on the fall equinox,
so on or around September 21.

On the fall equinox, there are as many hours of sunlight as there are of night, so Mabon is about seeking balance. On this night, we can show our respect for the darkness, since so many of the holidays are about honoring the sun. It is also a time to give thanks, to feel grateful for all that we have received this year.

WAYS TO CELEBRATE:

◆ Write a gratitude list, paying special attention to the things you might take for granted.

◆ Look up and read stories of death and rebirth—like those of Odin, Persephone, Mabon, Osiris, Mithras, Dionysus, and Jesus Christ.

◆ Throw a party! Mabon was traditionally a grand feast day.

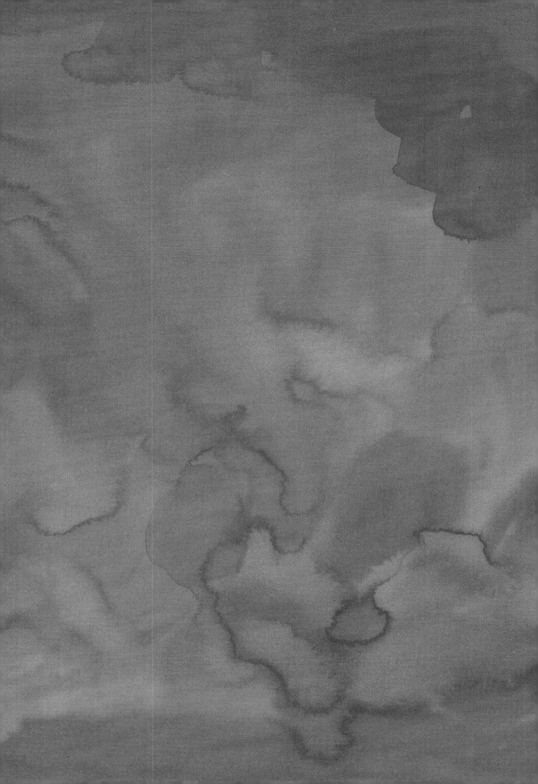

MAGIC SPELLS

· ·

WHAT DOES CASTING A SPELL EVEN LOOK LIKE?

It can look like whatever you want it to! Sometimes, casting a spell looks a lot like it does in the movies, though without the glowy purple or red swirly special effects. You can speak out loud, saying something that feels magical to you. You can hold stones or crystals or use herbs to make potions. It's all about what feels good and right for you.

But here are a few things you might try when you're thinking about how to cast a spell.

Purification

Take a bath before you cast a spell, with some lavender or sage floating in the water if you like the way they smell. This can get you in the right frame of mind and help you get rid of whatever energy you might be carrying—anything you don't want to bring to your spell. Meditate to clear your mind, as well as your body, by sitting quietly, breathing deeply, and letting your thoughts drift by.

Style

Dress however feels right to you—if wearing something fancy and witchy gets you in the mood, go for it! But remember that a T-shirt and jeans can be just as magical—what matters is your focus and intent.

Creating a Ritual Space

You can create a circle around you to show that you're about to work some magic. You can place stones in a circle, draw lines with chalk, or sprinkle salt. If you don't want to create a physical circle, you can create a mental one by walking in a circle with an herbal bundle or with a crystal selenite wand, drawing the circle in the air. If you can perform your spell outside, that's great—if not, open a window so you can feel the breeze.

Protection

Gathering and releasing power can bring all kinds of energy together, including some you might not want around. Protect yourself by placing holly, garlic, or betony close by, and use crystals like obsidian and black tourmaline, as well.

Invocation

If you like, you can call on the powers of someone or something, like Hecate, the goddess of witchcraft, or simply Spirit or the universe. Call on the support of your ancestors or someone you look up to. You can do this with a drawing or picture or just by thinking about them.

Casting

You can recite a special phrase, like those you'll find in the Basic Spells (see page 58), or simply state what you want to happen. Words only have as much power as you give them, but sometimes speaking a phrase out loud helps you feel more powerful in the same way that dressing "witchy" does—and if you *feel* more powerful, you *are* more powerful.

Giving Thanks

If you asked for help, be sure to say thank you! You can leave a gift or just bow your head in gratitude—whatever feels right to you.

Closing the Circle

It is important to *finish* your spells, and closing the circle lets the universe know that the spell is complete. If your circle was a mental one, take your herbal bundle or selenite wand and walk in the opposite direction. If you used stones to create the circle, collect them one by one, giving thanks. If you used salt or chalk, wash it away, again with thanks.

Will your spell work?

You are the only one who can decide that. It certainly won't work if you don't believe it will. But a spell might not work exactly the way you expect it to, for a lot of different reasons. Certain times of day are more powerful than others (sunrise, sunset, early evening, midnight), and certain times of the month are as well (new moon, full moon, etc.). If you're tired, or have trouble focusing your energies, your spell might not work as well.

Whatever you do, remember the Rule of Three: whatever you send out into the world will be returned to you, three times as powerfully.

BASIC SPELLS

Truth Spell

✳

Write your question on a piece of paper. Fold it toward yourself, over and over several times until it is as small as possible. Take a tigereye stone and hold it over the folded piece of paper. Focus on the stone and say the following incantation, or another one you like:

Let the truth be revealed
Clear away all deceit
Let nothing be concealed
So mote it be

Healing Spell

✳

Create your ritual space by using a garlic or sage herbal bundle, and have turquoise, garnet, and clear quartz on an altar or in your hands. Focus on the person you wish to heal. If you are the one who needs to be healed, place the stone or stones on the place where you're hurting, or if the person you wish to heal is with you, place the stones on their body. After you focus on your spot, imagine white light and energy flowing from your hand. Say the following incantation:

Let this pain ease
Let my power flow
Let this sickness cease
So mote it be

Protection Spell

✴

If you have something specific you want to protect yourself or someone else from, make a doll or some other symbol for it and place some protection stones around it. Use smoky quartz, obsidian, hematite, and pyrite. If it's a general protection spell, you don't need to make something specific—you can just hold your stones in your hands. Build an imaginary wall around yourself or the person you wish to protect in your mind. Hold tight to that image, and say this incantation:

Let no harm befall
Against all threats, be strong
Let (NAME) be safe behind my wall
So mote it be

Self-Confidence Spell

✳

Begin by writing on a small piece of paper something you already like about yourself or maybe something you want to feel more confident about. To create your ritual space, use an herbal bundle made out of thyme, sage, and lavender. Place aquamarine, azurite, moonstone, citrine, and obsidian in a circle around you. Hold your affirmation to your heart, and say the following incantation:

Let my true self shine through
I am already all that I need to be
*Let me **know** that this is true*
So mote it be

PART 3

DIVINATION

TAROT

• •

THERE'S NO REASON WHY TAROT SHOULD WORK—IT'S JUST A
deck of cards with pretty pictures on them—but somehow, every reading
has something real to say, something that makes you nod your head and
laugh a little at how true it feels. Most of the time, the feeling you get
after a reading is relief, like the cards agree with what you already knew.
Tarot cards tell you what you hope or think or fear, and then they advise
you: What do you want to do? What *should* you do? How will it all work
out?

Trying to get those answers is known as *divination*. The truth is that
divination happens when we use our intuition and listen to our hearts,
but there are certain tools that we can use to make divination a little easier—and tarot is one of them.

Back in the 1400s, the first tarot decks were used for playing card
games. It wasn't until the late 1700s that tarot was often used for divination; before that, fortune-tellers used simpler decks. Like playing cards,
tarot cards have four suits: Cups, Pentacles, Swords, and Wands. Cups
represent relationships, Pentacles represent work and money, Swords
are about conflict, and Wands are all about magic and creativity. The
suit cards have numbers 1 to 10 just like playing cards, and the "face
cards" are the Page, Knight, Queen, and King. These are known as the
Minor Arcana.

But a tarot deck has 22 more cards called the Major Arcana. They are arranged like a story, starting with the Fool, passing through Death and the Tower—which aren't as scary as you might think!—and ending with the World—a card of happy endings.

Even if you don't know a lot about tarot, you can do a reading, because like all magic, it's all about intention. The cards won't tell you anything you don't already know, because you are giving your energy to the cards and they are sharing it back to you. If you ask the cards a question, they will reflect the truth you already know inside, even if you aren't ready to admit it. Any power they have comes from what you bring to them.

Each tarot deck comes with a book that tells you the meaning of each card, and that's very helpful. But as you practice and get to know your deck, you'll find that each card has a slightly different, specific meaning that is special to you!

When it comes to choosing a deck, there are so many options it can feel overwhelming. The most common decks are the Rider-Waite (with artwork by Pamela Colman Smith—so her name is also included sometimes) or Aleister Crowley Thoth, but that doesn't mean that they will be the best for you. Look for a deck that makes you *want* to do a reading. A deck that you like is one that will give you the truest answers.

The more often you read tarot, the deeper and further you'll be able to see. Listen to your instincts.

THE SUITS

Cups

The suit of Cups is about relationships and how we feel about those relationships. When you see a spread with a lot of Cups, there is something going on with one of your relationships . . . but it might also mean that you are focusing more on your feelings than your thoughts.

This isn't always a bad thing—remember, there are no "bad" cards—but there can be challenges. Emotions are how we experience the world, but if we only listen to our feelings, we won't make good choices.

Pentacles

The suit of Pentacles—also known as Coins or Disks—is the suit of work and success. That could mean schoolwork, or it could be the work you do around the house, like chores or taking care of your siblings.

Pentacles is a very *practical* suit, which might seem funny in tarot—but at the same time, it's kind of nice to see our most basic needs and goals on the same level as our creativity and relationships. But if we pay too much attention to Pentacles, we can lose sight of the more important things in life.

Swords

✳

The suit of Swords is about conflict. We all get into fights and arguments with others sometimes, but Swords can also be about a conflict inside yourself, like when your thoughts and feelings don't agree. It's easy to want to run away from what they have to say. But the thing is, Swords are often right. Sometimes, our hearts can tell us something we *want* to be true, instead of what really *is* true. Swords give us cold, hard facts.

Remember, there are no "bad" cards, and this is not a "bad" suit. Looking at something with your mind instead of your heart is important, too, even when it is hard. Swords will keep you on the right track.

Wands

✳

The suit of Wands is about the magic we create—energy, intuition, and growth. Wands can help you bring your true self out into the open. In fact, you must be your true self when Wands are present—they want you to show everyone who you are. That can be scary, too, so it's important to balance Wands with the other three suits. But Wands help us pursue our creativity so that we can live a magical, powerful life.

THE MAJOR ARCANA

Here's a quick rundown of the individual Major Arcana cards so you can get a sense of their symbolism in readings. But remember your intuition is the key! What you see in the cards and their relationships in a reading will give you the answers you are looking for.

0 The Fool
✴

Idealism, Innocence, Potential. If the Fool is in your reading, try starting something new. Be free, and embrace the "foolishness" in yourself.

1 The Magician
✴

Mastery, Magic, Power. The Magician can do anything—and he will. This is a card of action, and it tells you that you can reach your goals.

2 The High Priestess
✴

Unconscious, Dreaming, Mystical. The High Priestess is the partner of the Magician. He steps forward with reason, and she steps back to let her intuition speak. Can you find the place between them?

3 The Empress
✴

Earth Mother, Creation, Fertility. The Empress is very caring. She tells you to support others, and yourself, especially through nature.

4 The Emperor

Tradition, Authority, Rules. The Emperor believes in
the importance of rules.

5 The Hierophant

Belief, Learning, Conformity. *Hierophant* is a word for an ancient priest who
held secret and special knowledge. The Hierophant believes in education,
but only known facts. Think of him like the Core Curriculum at school.

6 The Lovers

Duality, Love, Harmony. The Lovers are about all kinds of close relationships, but they can be about hard decisions where there doesn't seem to be
one right answer—because you want both together.

7 The Chariot

Balance, Self-Control, War Within. There are two animals (usually horses)
pulling the Chariot, and you must work out how to control both of them. If
you do, you will have success.

8 Strength

Resilience, Fortitude, Self-Confidence. If the Chariot is about control, true
Strength means being someone you and others can depend on. You must
have patience, compassion, and self-confidence.

9 The Hermit

Spirituality, Solitude, Wisdom. If the Hermit appears, it's time to look inside yourself. Give yourself some alone time to find answers.

10 Wheel of Fortune

Change, Destiny, Cycles. Change is the only constant in our lives, and the Wheel of Fortune shows how, with every year, we move forward.

11 Justice

Morality, Clear Distinctions, Karma. Justice turns up when you are trying to do the right thing—or when you feel you have been wronged.

12 The Hanged Man

Sacrifice, Self-Awareness, Knowledge. The Hanged Man demands something that seems impossible—that we show our strength by giving up control. He helps us learn to let go.

13 Death

Change, Transformation, Endings. The Death card can be scary, even though it doesn't mean actual death—don't worry about that! It's scary because it means change and change is hard. Something is coming to an end, and something new is beginning.

14 Temperance

Moderation, Compromise, Self-Control. So many cards in the tarot are about two sides of one thing, and Temperance is the most comforting of them. She brings opposite things together and teaches them to respect one another.

15 The Devil

Self-Deception, The Monster Within, Ignorance. If there *were* a "bad" card in tarot, the Devil would be it. But this card is really just about a bad situation—usually one you have created (perhaps accidentally). The Devil helps you look at your life to see where you have made mistakes and how you can grow from them.

16 The Tower

Destruction, Betrayal, Starting Over. If Death is about change, at least it's a change that we can see coming. The Tower changes all at once. It could mean looking at things in a new way—or it could mean a big life change.

17 The Star

Hope, Inspiration, New Possibilities. As hard as things can get, there is always a way out—there is always hope. When you see the Star, take a breath and allow the universe to calm and inspire you.

18 The Moon

Illusion, Mystery, Possibility. The world looks different by moonlight—and different can be a little scary sometimes. But it doesn't have to be. When the Moon is out, anything is possible—let your imagination wander. Allow the impossible.

19 The Sun

Clarity, Confidence, Surety. There is no reason to feel confused when you see the Sun—and you should feel joy in that. The Sun tells you that you are smart, energetic, and successful.

20 Judgment

Looking Back, Conviction, Redemption. Judgment can be about deciding if something is right or wrong, or you could instead use *good judgment* and think about the choices you have made.

21 The World

Completion, Fulfillment, Unity. The World completes the story of the tarot. You have finished what you set out to do, and you should celebrate the wholeness inside yourself.

HOW TO READ TAROT CARDS

What do you do with your tarot cards? Pulling them from the deck and laying them out is called a "spread," and there are many different kinds. We'll look at two to get you on your way.

past

my conscious

present

my subconscious

future

my focus

Three-Card Spread

One of the easiest spreads to start with is a three-card spread—that means a reading when you pull three cards from the deck. To start, have the person you're reading for shuffle the cards. Next, ask them to hold the deck close to their heart and ask their question. If they don't have a question, that's okay too, and if you're doing a reading for yourself, you can shuffle the cards for yourself.

Spread the cards out a little bit in your hand. Then have the person you're reading for choose three cards, or if you're reading for yourself, let your intuition help you choose. If the answer to your question feels like it is hiding, try to choose a hidden card. Sometimes your card will make your fingers tingle, or it might feel a little warm under your hands.

Lay the three cards faceup. Ask the cards from left to right: "What is going on in my life that I can see?" "What is going on in my life that I can't see?" and "What should I focus on today?"

Guidance Spread

This spread is a bit more complicated, but it can be really helpful when you have a specific problem or need to see all sides of whatever is going on. To start, shuffle and hold the cards close to your heart as you ask your question. You'll draw eight cards: the first by itself, and then seven in a row above it.

FIRST CARD ◆ This card shows the big idea for your reading.

SECOND CARD ◆ Why are you asking this question? What do you need help with?

THIRD CARD ◆ This card represents the area(s) in your life that you need advice on.

FOURTH CARD ◆ This card points out something you might not have noticed.

FIFTH CARD ◆ This card will give you the information you need.

SIXTH CARD ◆ This card will help you feel less worried.

SEVENTH CARD ◆ This card will help you move forward.

EIGHTH CARD ◆ This card tells you how it could all work out.

ASTROLOGY

• •

ARIES, TAURUS, GEMINI, CANCER, LEO, VIRGO, LIBRA, SCORPIO, Sagittarius, Capricorn, Aquarius, Pisces.

These are the signs of the zodiac, and you might already know which one belongs to you! Many people know their zodiac sign, which is based on when you were born, and like to read advice for their sign in horoscopes in newspapers, magazines, or online.

But sometimes, what goes into those horoscopes—the astrology behind it—can seem pretty confusing. There is a lot to keep track of, but it doesn't have to be too complicated! Astrology has been around for hundreds of years and it's simply about using the ways the stars and planets move and the various relationships between their attributes and characteristics to help figure out what might be going on here on earth.

The zodiac is a collection of 12 groupings of stars called constellations that the sun and the planets move through in the sky in the course of a year. Those 12 constellations each have their own personalities, and—you guessed it—those personalities shape what your individual zodiac sign means. So how do the signs get those personalities? Well, each sign is ruled by either the sun, the moon, or one of the planets, which each have their own personalities, too—even though all of these celestial bodies will visit each sign in the sky at some point. When we talk about the signs, we go in the order of the seasons, with spring coming first. The regular order of signs is the one at the beginning of this chapter.

Each sign also has an element that goes with it: fire, water, earth, or air. While every sign has its own personality traits, it will also have many traits in common with other signs that share the same element.

Just to be a little more confusing and add another piece to the puzzle, in astrology we also have 12 Houses, which have nothing to do with the 12 signs. Each House is an area of your life—like your family, your identity, and so on. The signs and the planets take turns moving through the Houses, so over the course of a year, each House will be "ruled" by a different sign and celestial body as these pass into and out of it. These come into play when you start to map out the relative positions of all the celestial bodies at a particular point in time.

So what does all of this mean for us? What does an astrological chart with the placement of all these parts do, anyway?

The most common astrological chart, the natal chart, shows where the stars were and what their positions mean in relation to the Houses on the day you were born. It's like a customized personality test, just for you, from the stars! It will give you an idea of what your life might be like, and maybe even a better understanding of who you are. But since your birthday is only one day—a very important day, but still just a single day—it is only a slice of the big picture. If you really start to love astrology, you can do a chart every month, week, or even day to help you make sense of what is going on in your life *right now* using the ever-shifting dance of all these pieces in the sky.

THE ELEMENTS AND THEIR SIGNS

Fire

✦

Fire Signs are powerful, energetic, and full of life. They are very creative, inspiring, and passionate, and they have big, strong feelings.

ARIES ✦ An Aries is a quick thinker and a born leader. Active and brave, they are competitive and energetic. Sometimes, they can be impatient or act without thinking first.

MARCH 21–APRIL 19 ✦ RULER: **Mars** ✦ GET ALONG WELL WITH: **Gemini**

LEO ✦ A Leo is creative and one of a kind. Passionate and generous, they love life and enjoy solving problems. Sometimes they might want to have all of the spotlight, instead of sharing it, because Leos love applause. Leos want to be seen for who they really are.

JULY 23–AUGUST 22 ✦ RULER: **Sun** ✦ GET ALONG WELL WITH: **Sagittarius**

SAGITTARIUS ✦ A Sagittarius wants to change the world. They love to think about big questions. They ask lots of questions and love to travel, but sometimes they can be impatient.

NOVEMBER 22–DECEMBER 21 ✦ RULER: **Jupiter** ✦
GET ALONG WELL WITH: **Leo**

Earth

Earth Signs get things done. They are responsible, loyal, patient, and work hard. They don't always like to try new things, but they have big goals and often get their way.

TAURUS ◆ A Taurus works hard and loves to enjoy the results of that work. They love beautiful things. They are stubborn, but in a good way, and will stick with a project—or a person—until the very end. Sometimes, Tauruses can be too stubborn and too protective.

APRIL 20–MAY 20 ✦ RULER: **Venus** ✦ GET ALONG WELL WITH: **Cancer**

VIRGO ◆ Kind and thoughtful, Virgos are very organized. They feel happy in nature. They can be shy and sometimes be too hard on themselves and others.

AUGUST 23–SEPTEMBER 22 ✦ RULER: **Mercury** ✦

BEST PAIRED WITH: **Scorpio**

CAPRICORN ◆ Capricorns are very independent. They are responsible and practical and hardly ever act without thinking first. Sometimes they find it hard to forgive others.

DECEMBER 22–JANUARY 19 ✦ RULER: **Saturn** ✦

BEST PAIRED WITH: **Pisces**

Air

✳

Air Signs are very smart and good at communication, but they also find it hard to sit still! They are always thinking about the next idea, and the next, looking for something new. They have lots of friends and love to talk, and they think the truth is the most important thing of all.

GEMINI ✦ A Gemini can be a little confusing, because sometimes they are fun and playful . . . and sometimes they are shy and have a hard time making choices. They are fascinated by the world and want to share what makes them happy with their friends and family.

MAY 21–JUNE 20 ✦ RULER: **Mercury** ✦ BEST PAIRED WITH: **Aries**

LIBRA ✦ Libras are peaceful and fair and love working together. They see the goodness and beauty in the world. A Libra might not love being alone and may be so afraid to have a fight that they let bad feelings grow, instead of talking it out.

SEPTEMBER 23–OCTOBER 22 ✦ RULER: **Venus** ✦

BEST PAIRED WITH: **Aquarius**

AQUARIUS ✦ Sometimes an Aquarius might seem shy, but they just like to spend a lot of time thinking. They are great at fixing problems and love to help others, but they also like to be alone. Sometimes they can be a little moody.

JANUARY 20–FEBRUARY 18 ✦ RULER: **Uranus** ✦ BEST PAIRED WITH: **Libra**

Water

✦

Water Signs are hard to predict, but they always have big, strong feelings—even if it doesn't always show. They are sensitive, intuitive, and kind, with big imaginations and independent spirits.

CANCER ✦ Like all Water Signs, Cancers care deeply—about their families most of all. They are very loyal and feel the pain of others. Sometimes it can be hard for Cancers to handle all their feelings.

JUNE 21–JULY 22 ✦ **RULER: Moon** ✦ **BEST PAIRED WITH: Taurus**

SCORPIO ✦ A Scorpio is strong-minded and isn't afraid to make decisions. They are great leaders and are good at sharing their emotions. They will keep your secrets—and are a little mysterious themselves. Sometimes, Scorpios can be a little jealous.

OCTOBER 23–NOVEMBER 21 ✦ **RULER: Mars** ✦
BEST PAIRED WITH: Virgo

PISCES ✦ Pisces are very friendly and caring—they are wonderful friends. They are wise and gentle and love to celebrate people's differences.

FEBRUARY 19–MARCH 20 ✦ **RULER: Neptune** ✦
BEST PAIRED WITH: Capricorn

THE CELESTIAL BODIES AND RULERS OF THE SIGNS

Sun

The Sun gives us light and life. It represents the power we have in our own lives. The Sun takes a trip through the zodiac once per year, spending about a month with each sign.

Moon

The Moon's light is full of mystery, and so the Moon is all about our intuition and deepest feelings. The Moon is tied to your family history and how you connect with your feelings. The Moon takes only 28 days to travel through the zodiac, spending two to three days with each sign.

Mercury

Mercury is great at communication, but mainly about concrete ideas instead of feelings. Mercury is all about research, learning, decision-making, and sharing what you know with others. When Mercury goes retrograde—meaning it looks like it is moving backward across the night sky even though it isn't really—it scrambles communications and causes all sorts of problems. If Mercury is in retrograde, try not to make any big decisions. Mercury retrograde also does strange things to technology, so don't be surprised if your phone or computer starts acting a little funny. Since Mercury is so close to the Sun, it takes about a year to travel the zodiac.

Venus

If you like mythology, you might have already guessed that Venus represents love, beauty, and the things that make you happy. Venus doesn't care that much about consequences or thinking things through—it's all about joy and fun. Venus takes about 10–12 months to travel across the zodiac, spending a few weeks with each sign.

Mars

Mars is a force of nature! Its energy is aggressive, competitive, and brave. Mars is in charge of war, but also all kinds of contests and conflicts, like sports and arguments. Mars takes about two years to circle the zodiac, spending six or seven weeks with each sign.

Jupiter

Jupiter is a planet of big ideas, hopefulness, and wisdom. As our largest gas giant, it casts a powerful shadow of good fortune—because of this, Jupiter is sometimes known as the Great Benefactor. Jupiter inspires us to try something new. Jupiter takes 12 years to travel the zodiac, and it sits with each sign for a full year.

Saturn

Called the Great Teacher, Saturn is a planet of ambition and hard work, but also of caution and responsibility. Saturn is not a dreamer;

instead it values patience and structure. Saturn takes 29 years to go across the zodiac and stays in each sign for two and a half years.

Uranus

If Saturn teaches us to be responsible and think things through, Uranus helps us learn to love surprises. It rules the future and all new technology. Uranus inspires us to think in new ways—maybe even ways that have never been thought of before! Uranus takes 84 years to circle the zodiac and stays with a sign for seven of those years—making those seven years very creative, indeed.

Neptune

Lovely Neptune is the planet of inspiration. Like the Moon, it governs intuition, dreams, the subconscious, and magic. But Neptune goes deeper than the Moon does, inspiring us to be more than we think we can be. Neptune circles the zodiac over the course of 146 years, staying with each sign for 14 years.

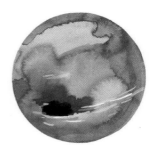

THE 12 HOUSES

FIRST HOUSE ◆ The House of the Self. It includes your personality, your body, how you look, and how you see yourself. The First House will tell you your Ascendant or Rising Sign, which is the sign that was just coming up over the horizon (where the sky meets the earth) when you were born. This sign can be just as important as your birth sign when it comes to understanding who you are. It represents the public face you show the world.

SECOND HOUSE ◆ The House of Worth. The sign that rests in your Second House tells you about the objects and things that are important to you and how you feel about them. Are you someone who is really careful with your stuff and saves your money? Or are you more carefree, making choices in the moment?

THIRD HOUSE ◆ The House of Intellect. It influences how you communicate with others and how you understand the world. It also refers to your neighborhood or hometown, and maybe short journeys away from home.

FOURTH HOUSE ◆ The House of the Home. It includes your house—where it is, what it looks like—and the things that make it your home, like your parents, your pets, your siblings, or other people you share space with.

FIFTH HOUSE ◆ The House of Love. It includes love of all kinds—for friends, family, and yourself—and it also rules creativity and self-expression.

SIXTH HOUSE ◆ The House of Work. It includes schoolwork, but also the work that you do in your daily life—like your chores. Exercise and healthy eating fall under this category, too, because they are the work we do to maintain our bodies.

SEVENTH HOUSE ◆ The House of Partnership. This usually means the most important person in your life, whether that's your best friend, a sibling, a parent, or someone else you care about a lot. Sometimes those relationships have conflicts, and this House deals with those as well.

EIGHTH HOUSE ◆ The House of Transformation. This House is about how we get along with the people we meet and talk with, and how those people change us.

NINTH HOUSE ◆ The House of Understanding. The Ninth House looks after dreams, visions, ideas, and rituals. Travel to faraway places, distant relatives, and education all belong to this House.

TENTH HOUSE ◆ The House of Status. The Tenth House helps us understand how our friends and other people might see us. This is the version of ourselves we show to others.

ELEVENTH HOUSE ◆ The House of Friendship. This House is about community and friendships as a group, instead of your relationship with a specific person.

TWELFTH HOUSE ◆ The House of the Subconscious. If the First House is about how you see yourself, the Twelfth House is about the side of you that you might not always see. It rules our dreams and our intuition, as well as our secrets and our sadness.

HOW TO CREATE
A NATAL CHART

For a detailed natal chart, you'll need the help of a professional—or you can even go online, where there are lots of free resources. But you can give it a try at home and still learn plenty of things about how the zodiac signs influence the Houses.

1. Draw a small circle on a piece of paper. Then draw a larger circle around that, and an even bigger one around your second circle. You should have three in total. Using a ruler, divide the circle into 12 equal parts, like you're slicing a pizza into 12 pieces.

2. Next, you will want to figure out your Ascendant Sign. Remember, your Ascendant Sign is whatever was rising over the horizon on the date and at the exact time of your birth, so you can ask your parents for that info and then use it to look up your Ascendant Sign online. This is your First House. You will want to put it in the slice of the pizza that matches where you would find the 8 on a clock.

3. From there, you can fill out the sections around the chart, going clockwise. Follow the order of the signs (see page 77) as you fill in the other 11 spaces. So if you had Aries in your First House, you would put Taurus in the Second House, Gemini in the Third House, and so on until you get all the way around.

What does all this tell you? Well, a lot! It can help explain why some parts of horoscopes might feel very true to you, and other parts don't quite fit. Let's look at an example. If you're a Libra, but your Ascendant Sign is Gemini, that might explain why some of the personality traits for your sign haven't felt quite right—because you're really a combination of both. (How exciting and special that makes you!) If you have Taurus in your Second House, then you might understand why you're so good at saving your money. If your Fifth House is ruled by Capricorn, it might explain why you can sometimes be stubborn, getting into fights with the people you love the most.

Or it might tell you nothing you don't already know! But it's still a lot of fun, and something to do on a rainy day.

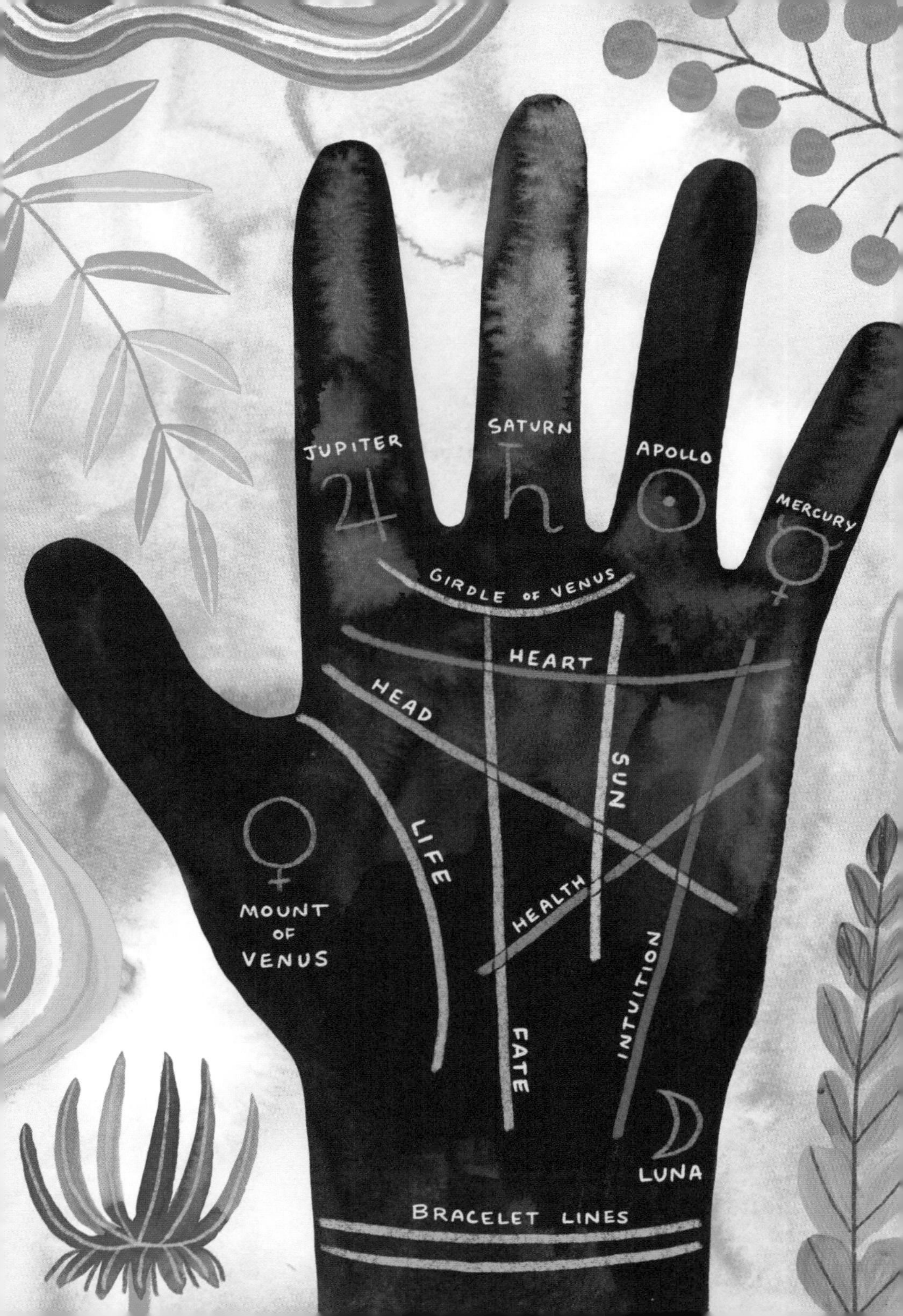
JUPITER
SATURN
APOLLO
MERCURY
GIRDLE OF VENUS
HEART
HEAD
SUN
LIFE
HEALTH
MOUNT OF VENUS
INTUITION
FATE
LUNA
BRACELET LINES

PALM-READING

PEOPLE HAVE BEEN READING PALMS FOR A REALLY LONG TIME! Thousands of years ago, people were reading palms in Babylonia, ancient Greece, China, India, and many other places. Like tarot and astrology, palmistry tells a lot about a person's personality, and less about their future—though there is a little of that sprinkled in, too!

Even if it can't share with us everything about the future, there is *something* happening with palm-reading. Our entirely unique fingerprints remind us that no two hands are exactly alike, even for people who are related. We do *everything* with our hands, and they show it. The callus from where you hold your pen, the way you bite your nails, scars from when you fell down trying to ride a skateboard—all of that is right there on your hands.

In palm-reading, also known as *chiromancy*, each hand will tell the person reading it something different. The nondominant hand—the one you don't use for writing or catching a ball—shows the things you were born with. The dominant hand—the one you use the most for everyday things—shows your life experience. Watch for the differences between the two hands.

UNDERSTANDING CHIROMANCY

There are three major lines on your hand—the life line, the heart line, and the head line—and several minor lines, plus some bumps and smudges that palm readers call mounts and markings. In the next few pages, you'll see different descriptions for these parts of the hand, and sometimes you'll find that a part of your hand matches more than one. For example, your life line might be short, forked, and shallow. The art of palmistry is not just in being able to see the lines clearly, but also learning how to understand and share what you see. Once you practice palm-reading, you might be able to tell that person with a short, forked, and shallow life line that they are better at dealing with hard things than they think they are and that they will need to use that ability soon because their life is about to change.

Each hand will have different lines, and when you're doing a reading, you'll want to look at both of them. Here's a tip to get you started: usually the nondominant hand will reveal more truths about the person.

THE MAJOR LINES

The Life Line

✳

This line contains so much information about your life—but it doesn't tell you when you are going to die, or anything scary like that. Instead, the life line describes the *kind* of life you will have and are having.

- ◆ **LONG.** A long life line means a healthy person.
- ◆ **SHORT.** A short life line means that the person is good at getting past challenges. Note: Does *not* mean a short life.
- ◆ **FAINT.** Low energy, maybe afraid to take chances.
- ◆ **DEEP.** A smooth and easy life.
- ◆ **BROKEN.** A life line with a break in it means that there has been or will be a major change in life. The closer to the wrist the break is, the earlier in the person's life the change will occur.
- ◆ **FORKED.** A fork means a change in lifestyle.
- ◆ **CHAINED.** Crisscrossing lines mean some challenges ahead.
- ◆ **MULTIPLES.** If the person has more than one life line moving along the same path, that can mean they have a true soul-partner in life, like a best friend.

The Heart Line

Also known as the love line, it can tell you about the person's emotions, as well as their relationships with others.

- **LONG.** Balanced and open, happy.

- **OVEREXTENDED.** If the line reaches all the way across the palm, that means the person might have trouble standing up for themselves.

- **SHORT.** A little selfish.

- **DEEP.** Stressed by relationships.

- **FAINT.** Emotions and relationships aren't that important to them.

- **STRAIGHT.** Likes to let others take charge in relationships.

- **CURVED.** Emotional, intuitive.

- **WAVY.** Impulsive.

- **BROKEN.** This person might have had, or will soon have, some emotional challenges.

- **FORKED.** Practical, good at maintaining balance.

- **CHAINED.** Feelings are easily hurt.

- **BRANCHES GOING UP.** Has strong relationships.

- **BRANCHES GOING DOWN.** Deals with heartbreak sometimes.

The Head Line

✦

The line of wisdom goes deeper than just learning—it's also about how the person thinks and gives an idea of their intuitive abilities.

- ◆ **STARTS FROM SAME POINT AS LIFE LINE.** Means they have a strong will.

- ◆ **LONG.** Means they are intelligent, have a good memory, and usually think things through.

- ◆ **OVEREXTENDED.** If the line reaches across the entire palm, the person is probably very successful and brave—though they might also be a little selfish.

- ◆ **SHORT.** Practical, no-nonsense.

- ◆ **STRAIGHT.** Realistic, good attention to detail. More practical than imaginative.

- ◆ **CURVED.** Intuitive and imaginative.

- ◆ **WAVY.** This person might be hard to trust, because their thoughts and actions don't always match up.

- ◆ **DEEP.** Sensible, with an excellent memory.

- ◆ **FAINT.** Daydreams, has trouble concentrating.

- ◆ **BROKEN.** This person might be mentally tired.

- ◆ **FORKED.** Called a "writer's fork" or a "lawyer's fork." The person enjoys debate, has an excellent imagination, and communicates clearly.

- **BRANCHES GOING UP.** Successful in work or school.

- **BRANCHES GOING DOWN.** This person has had a struggle or disappointment in the past.

THE MINOR LINES

Not all of these lines will be present for every person, but some of them may be. There are many minor lines, even beyond these, but they are the most common ones.

- **SUN LINE.** Also known as the Apollo line. This person is creative, successful, and self-confident.

- **BRACELET LINES.** Also known as rascette lines. The more of these lines someone has, and the clearer those lines are, the longer and healthier that person's life will be.

- **FATE LINE.** Also known as the line of destiny. This line points out events that the person has no control over and challenges that must be faced.

- **GIRDLE OF VENUS.** This person has a lot of feelings. It is someone who can be very happy and also very sad.

- **LINE OF HEALTH.** Might say something about the person's health, but probably more about their skills as a healer of other people.

◆ **INTUITION LINE.** This person is very sensitive and may even have psychic abilities. Doesn't like being in crowds.

MOUNTS

Mounts are the bumps of flesh on the palms.

◆ **MOUNT OF VENUS.** The person is healthy, has positive relationships, and sees the beauty in the world.

◆ **MOUNT OF JUPITER.** The person is kind and generous and has a positive attitude.

◆ **MOUNT OF SATURN.** The person is friendly and independent and takes their responsibilities seriously.

◆ **MOUNT OF APOLLO.** Also known of the Mount of the Sun. The person is adventurous and goes with the flow.

◆ **MOUNT OF MERCURY.** The person is good at communication.

◆ **MOUNT OF LUNA.** Also known as the Mount of the Moon. The person is artistic and is happiest when they are in nature, particularly by the sea.

MARKINGS

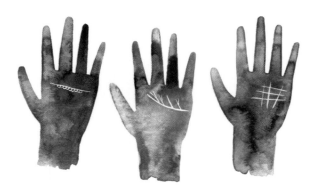

Of course, we all have other marks all over our hands, sometimes on the lines themselves. These add a deeper layer of meaning to the lines, helping you get more specific in your interpretations.

- ◆ **BREAKS.** Most lines have breaks in them, and they don't necessarily mean anything bad—it's more like a break in the flow of energy in those lines, which happens to all of us.

- ◆ **CHAINS.** Chains in a line can mean obstacles, the things we must get past as we move forward in life.

- ◆ **TRIDENT, TRIANGLE.** These markings are signs of good luck.

- ◆ **FRAY.** When a line ends in a fray, that can mean uncertainty—life lines often end in frays, as we never know for sure how life will go.

- ◆ **ISLANDS.** An island represents a difficult time in the person's life.

- ◆ **GRILLES.** These can mean stress.

- ◆ **CROSSES.** Even more stress, like "a cross to bear."

HOW TO DO
A READING

Look at the person's nondominant hand first. This will help you read the differences in the dominant hand. Take your time—there is a lot to look at and pay attention to. Take notes if you want!

Next, look at the person's dominant hand. For now, don't worry about comparing the two, just see what the dominant hand tells you.

Finally, compare the two, and see the differences between them. If lines are clearer on one hand than the other, what does that tell you? If some markings are present on one hand, but not the other, what does that mean? For instance, if the fate line is present on the nondominant hand, but missing on the dominant hand, maybe that person has stepped aside from whatever destiny had in store for them.

When you think you have learned all that you can, share your thoughts with the person whose hands you have been studying. Walk them through the process, and see how much of it rings true to them.

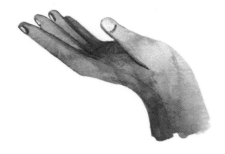

DREAM
INTERPRETATION

. . . .

WE ALL DREAM. WE MAY NOT ALL *REMEMBER* OUR DREAMS, BUT we all have them. And sometimes our dreams can be pretty weird! There are dreams so intense that we feel they *must* be important in some way. Have you ever woken up from a dream wondering what on earth your unconscious was trying to tell you? In this chapter, we'll start to find out.

How and why we dream aren't certain, but oneirologists (dream scientists) agree that dreams help us form memories, process emotions, and sort through what happened during the day. Some folks believe that dreams are messages sent to us from the beyond or that they show us things that happened in our past lives. There are traditions of dream interpretation in Islam, Christianity, Hinduism, and Buddhism, with many symbols shared between them.

Symbols are the language of dreams, and each thing you see in your dreams has a specific meaning. A dream dictionary could tell you that dreaming of a fern shows your hopes and fears for the future . . . but it might not mean that for you. Instead, you might dream of a fern because your grandmother kept ferns in her house and you're missing her. Dreams have meanings that are specific to every individual person. They're special and unique.

But oneirologists *have* noticed trends, and there are lots of dreams that happen to almost every one of us at some point—often more than once—in different cultures all over the world. Like dreams of going to school naked or flying or falling—we all have dreams like these. And because they are so common, we are able to interpret them and figure that they all mean pretty much the same thing for everyone. Just like yawning probably means you're sleepy and smiling probably means you're happy, no matter who is doing the yawning or the smiling, these common dreams usually indicate the same thing for everyone.

And while the less common dream symbols don't always carry the same message, those general interpretations can still be useful. Say you've had an upsetting dream, and you just can't stop thinking about it. Sometimes, if you can understand the dream, you can let it go, and dream symbols can help you begin to interpret it. Dream dictionaries have thousands of symbols—some of them as common as mothers, and some as weird as ice makers. Who dreams about ice makers? But if you do, then it might mean that you are shutting others out, closing yourself off from your friends and family—and whether this sounds right to you or not, it is interesting to think about.

Dreams have meaning, and if we look at them closely, we can come to understand them as best we can so that we may better understand ourselves.

COMMON DREAM SYMBOLS

Most likely, you've dreamed each of these at least once.

Being Chased

We remember these dreams because we feel so much anxiety during them. To try to interpret a dream like this, take a look at what is chasing you. What might that symbolize for you? What is it you are having trouble facing? Your dream is telling you to *stop running*.

Falling

Normally, dreams of falling happen after you've achieved something you were working toward. They're about being afraid of *what's next*. What will you do now?

Water

In a lot of cultures, water is a symbol of the unconscious. If you're dreaming of a stormy sea, maybe your emotions have been a little stormy lately, too. But if you're dreaming of a cool, clear stream, you are probably thinking clearly.

Test You Didn't Study For

✦

This dream could be a concern about a specific class, but it might also mean that you are wishing you had made some different choices.

Death

✦

Much like in tarot, these dreams do not mean literal death. Don't worry if you dream about dying—you're not sick, and nobody you love is in danger. Instead, the dream might mean that things are about to change—something is about end, and something else is about to begin.

Flying

✦

These dreams are usually amazing, just so much fun, and they often happen after we have finally made a decision we've been avoiding or when we're feeling confident and things are going well in our lives.

Nudity

✦

We've all suffered from the "forgot your clothes" dream. This unpleasant dream usually means you're feeling unsafe. Maybe you're worried people won't like the real you. Get it over with and really put your true self out there for the world to see.

LESS COMMON (BUT STILL FAIRLY COMMON) DREAM SYMBOLS

These show up less frequently,
but they are still more common than an ice maker!

Celebrities

When a famous person pops up in your dream, that might mean that they are showing you a part of yourself that is like them in some way. So if there's an actor you think is really funny, that might mean that *you* are really funny, too.

Food

Dreaming of food can mean that you are hungry, but it can also mean you are hungry to learn.

House

The house itself is you, and each room or floor of the house has a meaning that is specific to you. Usually, a basement represents something you've been ignoring, and a bedroom represents something private, maybe a secret.

Killing

✦

If you kill someone in your dreams, that doesn't make you a violent person. Every character in your dream represents a part of yourself. So if you have this dream, think about what part of yourself you might be ready to let go of.

Needing to Go to the Bathroom

✦

This probably just means that you need to go to the bathroom, but it could also mean that you should pay attention to your own needs, instead of always putting others first.

Teeth Falling Out

✦

Teeth symbolize confidence and power. If you're dreaming of your teeth falling out, ask yourself what you might be feeling powerless about. We also use our teeth to communicate—what have you been wanting to say to someone, but you feel like you can't?

Snakes

✦

The symbolism of snakes in dreams depends on how you feel about snakes. If you dislike them or are afraid of them, dreaming of snakes may be about something you're scared of. But they can also represent healing, change, and creativity.

HOW TO
INTERPRET DREAMS

Start by keeping a dream journal. Write down every dream you remember when you first wake up in the morning, paying attention to any details that jump out at you. If you have the same dream over and over, or if you dream of the same place over and over, then that's probably pretty important.

At the end of the day, before you go to sleep, write about what's on your mind. This is just a good habit to get into—it lets you clear your mind for restful sleep. But it will also help you to see how the events of the day might have an impact on your dreams that night.

As you do this, you'll start to notice patterns, and symbols that repeat will start to make more sense to you.

If you're interpreting someone else's dream, listen carefully and patiently. Other people's dreams are never as interesting as our own, but do your best. If you notice any particular symbols, make note of them. Ask them some questions about what might be going on in their life so that you can interpret more clearly. When you're ready to tell them what you think, let them know that this isn't an exact science, and you can't know for sure—dreams are very personal, and even if someone has asked you to interpret, they may not like what you have to say. Just give them your honest opinion.

LUCID DREAMS

You know how sometimes, when you're dreaming, you *know* that you're dreaming? That's a lucid dream, and sometimes with practice, when you know that you are dreaming, you can start to control your dreams.

Why would you want to do that? Well, for starters, it's really *fun*. You can do anything you want! You can fly, you can work magic, you can save the world.

So the first thing you need to do is to get better at realizing that you're dreaming while it's happening. Keeping a dream journal will help with this. So will paying attention to your dreams and thinking about them when you're awake. Work on remembering them. When you wake up from a dream, even if it is the middle of the night, take the time to write it down, or try to remember it from start to finish. Note as many details as you can, so you can write it down later.

The best time to lucid dream is when you are just barely asleep—in the early morning or during a nap, for example. If you wake up out of a dream in the early morning, pay attention to that dream as closely as you can, while letting your mind stay as relaxed as possible. Daydream the dream over again. And then, once you've decided how you want the dream to go, let yourself fall back asleep. It may be a very light sleep, but you will find yourself dreaming the daydream.

CONCLUSION

EVERYTHING WE'VE COVERED IS JUST MEANT TO GET YOU started. There is *so much more* to learn and explore in the world of magic. But remember, as you study and research and seek new mystical knowledge and power, the most powerful source is within yourself.

Each of these paths—healing, magic, and divination—was founded by ancient magical practitioners long ago, and each of them started with someone wondering *what if?* They began with curiosity, a sense of adventure, and above all, a willingness to be creative and to listen to their own intuition. You can always create your own magic using only what you carry within you.

If you laugh at the idea of casting spells and think that sitting down and trying to do one would just be embarrassing, then that might not be the kind of magic that's right for you! You might work your magic using art, music, or simply a whisper of intention on the wind. Pull that tarot card, and see what it says. Study the lines on your palm to learn more about who you are and who you want to be. What can your natal chart tell you about how you handle certain situations, and how can you use that information to handle them even better?

All that matters is what we believe is possible. If we open up to the potential of magic, it can become real, practical, and true. We make it so, and so mote it be.

GLOSSARY

ASCENDANT SIGN. Also known as "Rising Sign," this is the sign or constellation that was coming up over the horizon at the time of your birth. It represents the version of yourself that you show to the world.

ASTROLOGICAL HOUSES. Twelve areas of your life, including family, friends, and identity, that can be guided by the zodiac.

ASTROLOGY. An ancient study of the planets and how they affect life on earth.

AURA. The energy that surrounds each living thing. Contains seven layers called the "subtle bodies."

CHAKRAS. Energy centers within your body. There are seven chakras: Muladhara (the root chakra), Svadhisthana (the sacral chakra), Manipura (the solar plexus chakra), Anahata (the heart chakra), Vishuddha (the throat chakra), Ajna (the third eye chakra), and Sahasrara (the crown chakra).

CHARM BAG. Also known as a spell bag, this is a physical representation of a spell.

CHIROMANCY. The study of the lines on the palm.

DIVINATION. The art of seeing into the future or into something hidden.

ELEMENTS. There are four basic elements in witchcraft and in astrology: earth, air, fire, and water.

HERB MAGIC. The practice of incorporating plants into your craft; a specialty of hearth or hedge witches. Often used for healing.

HERBAL BUNDLE. Herbs dried into a small bunch. Intended to be lit on fire and allowed to smolder, sending its smoke and essence into the air.

HERBAL OIL. Herbs steeped in oil to preserve their scent and magical properties.

LUCID DREAMING. The practice of controlling your dreams while you are dreaming them.

MAGICAL HOLIDAYS. Ancient holidays that celebrate the seasons and the harvest. Include Samhain, Yule, Imbolc, Ostara, Beltane, Litha, Lammas, and Mabon.

MEDITATION. A practice of sitting quietly and breathing deeply that allows your mind to rest.

MERCURY RETROGRADE. When Mercury's orbit appears to be heading backward across the sky, which can affect electronics and communication.

NATAL CHART. Your personal chart of the 12 Astrological Houses.

ONEIROLOGY. The study of dreams.

PALMISTRY. The study of the lines and other markers on the hands for divination.

PRANA. Also known as "qi," this is the energy or life force that runs through the body.

RULE OF THREE. A basic standard of witchcraft; it states that whatever you send out into the world will be returned to you threefold.

SO MOTE IT BE. A traditional magical phrase that means "make it so" and serves to center your magical intention on an outcome.

TAROT. A divination practice using a deck of cards with special meanings.

ZODIAC. The 12 constellations that make up our astrological horoscope.

ACKNOWLEDGMENTS

THIS WAS A WORK OF MANY HANDS! THANK YOU FIRST AND FORE-most to Shannon Fabricant, for helping bring more magic into the lives of young witches. Also to Julie Matysik, Amber Morris, and the fabu-lously magical Ashley Benning! Thank you to Katie Vernon for always and ever the prettiest books in the land. Thank you to Valerie Howlett and Isabella Nugent and the whole incredible team at RP Kids—I'm so lucky to be a part of your amazing family.

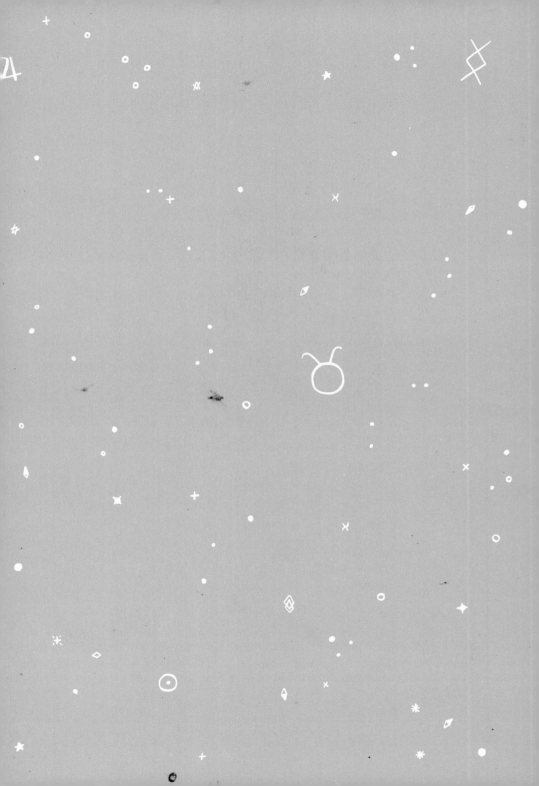